AF541601
Must Know 100 Facts about the
BIRDS
Om Books International

First Published in 2025 by

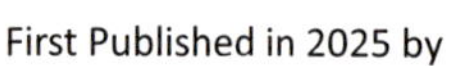

Om Books International

Corporate & Editorial Office
A-12, Sector 64, Noida 201 301
Uttar Pradesh, India
Phone: +91 120 477 4100
Email: editorial@ombooks.com
Website: www.ombooksinternational.com

Sales Office
107, Ansari Road, Darya Ganj
New Delhi 110 002, India
Phone: +91 11 4000 9000
Email: sales@ombooks.com
Website: www.ombooks.com

ISBN: 978-93-52761-75-3

Printed in India

10 9 8 7 6 5 4 3 2 1

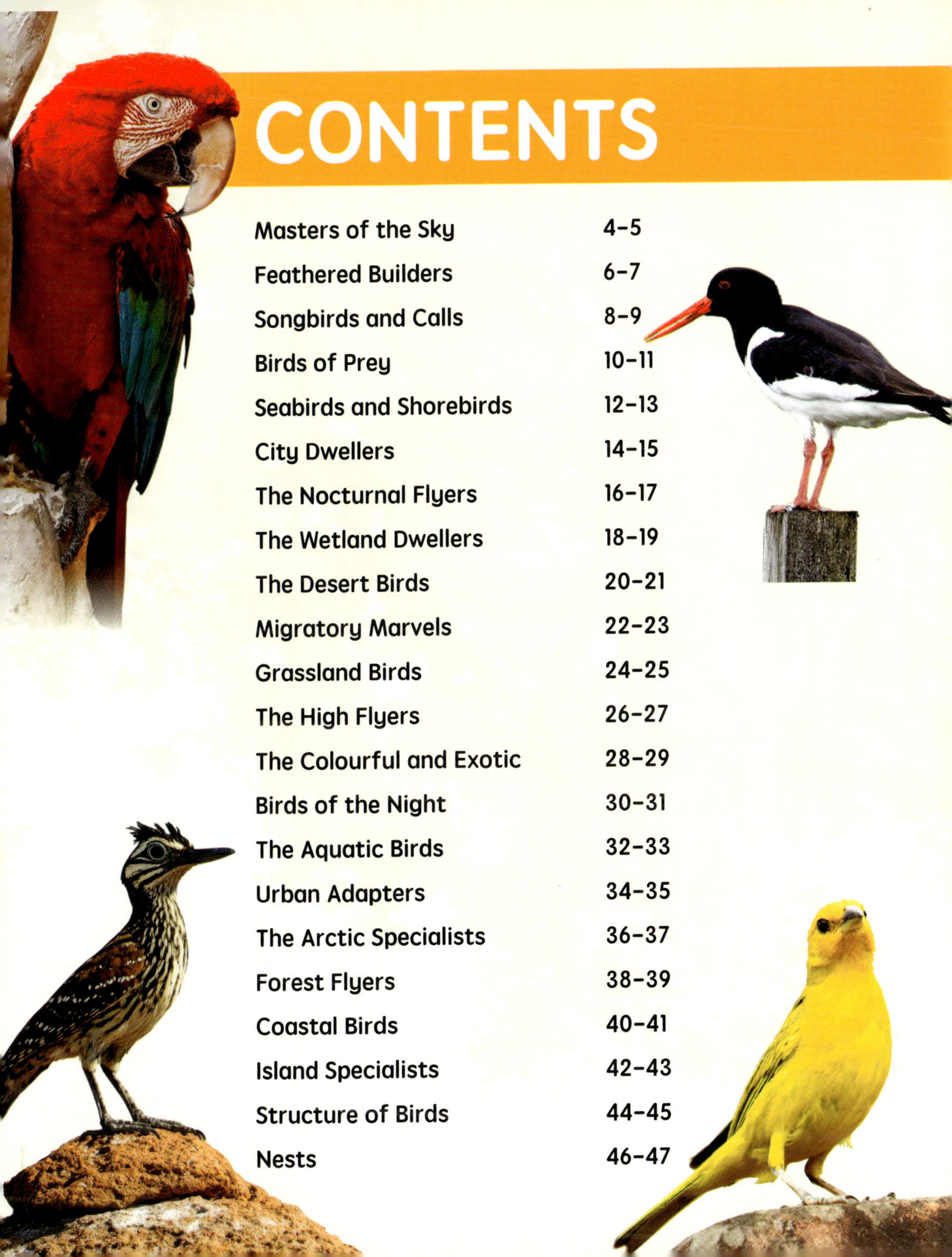

CONTENTS

MASTERS OF THE SKY

THE PEREGRINE FALCON: FAST AND FURIOUS

The peregrine falcon is the fastest bird, flying as fast as 320 km/h (200 mph) when it dives to catch its prey.

Fun Fact

A group of flamingos is known as a flamboyance.

ALBATROSS: THE LONG-DISTANCE TRAVELLER

The wandering albatross has the longest wingspan of any living bird, which can stretch up to 3.5 metres (11.5 feet).

THE SWIFT'S SKY ADVENTURES

Common swifts spend most of their lives flying in the air. They only land to build their nests. They eat and sleep, and have babies during flight.

HUMMINGBIRDS: TINY FLYING MASTERS

Hummingbirds are the only birds that can fly backwards. Their unique wing structure allows them to hover around quickly.

EAGLES: STRONG AND SHARP-EYED HUNTERS

Eagles are among the world's largest birds of prey, known for their powerful build and keen eyesight, which can spot a rabbit up to two miles away.

FEATHERED BUILDERS

WEAVER BIRDS: NATURE'S NEST BUILDERS

Weaver birds create beautiful nests by weaving grass and leaves. They do this to impress other birds.

Fun Fact

Some species of male frigate birds inflate their red throat pouches to the size of a balloon to attract partners.

THE BOWERBIRD'S COLOURFUL DISPLAY

Male bowerbirds build complex nests, decorated with brightly coloured objects, to impress other birds.

WOODPECKERS: THE CARPENTERS OF THE FOREST

Woodpeckers are known for their ability to drill into trees to find food or make nests. They use their strong beaks and heads to do it.

MONTEZUMA OROPENDOLA: MASTERNEST BUILDERS

They build hanging nests that can be over a metre long. They hang from the ends of tree branches to protect the birds from predators.

FLAMINGO MUD TOWERS

Flamingos build high mud mounds for their nests. The mounds help regulate temperature and keep eggs safe from flooding and predators.

SONGBIRDS AND CALLS

Fun Fact

The Eurasian skylark can sing for hours, often while flying.

THE LYREBIRD: THE MASTER MIMICKER

The superb lyrebird can mimic almost any sound it hears, including chainsaws, car alarms, and other bird calls.

CANARIES: THE SINGING SENSATIONS

Canaries were once regularly used in coal mines to detect toxic gases. They are celebrated for their melodious songs.

THE WHISTLING PIGEON

Some species of pigeons make a whistling sound with their wings when they fly, which is believed to be a form of communication.

THE NIGHTINGALE'S TIMELESS TUNES

Nightingales are famous for their powerful and beautiful songs that have inspired poets and musicians for centuries.

CROWS: SKILLFUL TALKERS

Crows can mimic human speech and a variety of other sounds, showing how smart they are with their voices.

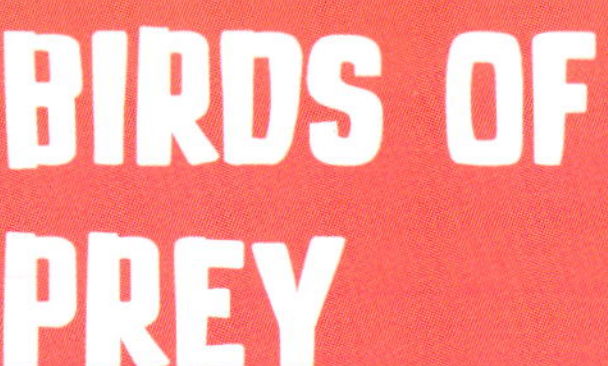

BIRDS OF PREY

THE OWL'S SILENT FLIGHT

Owls have special feathers that make no noise when they fly, allowing them to approach their prey almost silently.

Fun Fact

The harpy eagle, one of the largest and most powerful eagles, has back claws called talons as long as a grizzly bear's claws.

HAWKS: PRECISION HUNTERS

Hawks have a keen sense of vision that allows them to spot their prey from far away.

OSPREYS: FISH SPECIALISTS

Ospreys are expert fish hunters.They have special toes that can turn around and hooked pads on their feet to help grip their slippery fish.

VULTURES: THE CLEAN-UP CREW

Vultures help nature by eating dead animals. This keeps the environment clean and also stops diseases from spreading.

KESTRELS: HOVERING HUNTERS

Kestrels can hover in mid-air while scanning the ground for small prey. This is known as 'wind-hovering'.

SEABIRDS AND SHOREBIRDS

PENGUINS:
THE ANTARCTIC DIVERS

Penguins are excellent swimmers. Their body shape, strong flippers, and webbed feet help them move easily in the water.

Fun Fact

Gannets use special air sacs to help them land safely when they dive from high altitudes into the sea.

ALBATROSS:
OCEAN GLIDERS

Albatrosses use the wind to travel thousands of miles across the ocean without flapping their wings.

PUFFINS: CLOWNS OF THE SEA

Puffins are often called 'sea parrots' because of their colourful beaks and waddling walk. They are among the world's favourite seabirds.

THE GANNET'S PLUNGE

Gannets dive from high altitudes into the sea at speeds of up to 100 km/h (62 mph) to catch fish.

SANDPIPERS: THE LONG-DISTANCE TRAVELLERS

Some sandpipers fly from the Arctic to the southern tip of South America. It is one of the longest trips any bird makes.

CITY DWELLERS

PIGEONS: CITY BIRDS

Pigeons, also known as rock doves, have learned to live in cities. They use building ledges instead of natural cliffs to build their nests.

Fun Fact

A large crow measures around 0.5 metres in length with a wingspan of up to 1 metre.

CROWS: SMART SURVIVORS

Crows are very intelligent. They have adapted well to live in cities. They use traffic to crack open nuts and even make tools to get food.

SPARROWS: ALWAYS AROUND

House sparrows are found in nearly every city around the world. They survive on the crumbs and shelters provided by humans.

BLACKBIRDS: THE GARDEN DWELLERS

Common blackbirds live in many gardens. They enjoy the food and places to build their nests in suburban areas.

THE ADAPTABILITY OF THE STARLING

Starlings are known for adjusting in different places. They can outsmart local birds in cities.

THE NOCTURNAL FLYERS

NIGHTHAWKS: NIGHTTIME FLYERS

Nighthawks are not actually hawks. They are nocturnal birds that catch insects while flying at dusk and dawn.

Fun Fact

Kakapos are the world's only flightless parrots. They are also among the rarest and most endangered because of their nocturnal habits.

NIGHTJARS: MASTERS OF DISGUISE

Nightjars are birds with feathers that help them blend in. They nest on the ground and are almost invisible among leaves or tree bark.

THE ENIGMATIC KIWI

Kiwis, the national symbol of New Zealand, are unique nocturnal birds. They have a keen sense of smell. They are the only birds with nostrils at the tip of their beak.

KAKAPO: THE NIGHT PARROT

The kakapo is a nocturnal parrot from New Zealand that can't fly. It has a friendly personality.

OWLET-NIGHTJARS: SMALL AND ELUSIVE

These small, nocturnal birds with soft feathers. They are great at moving through thick forests.

THE WETLAND DWELLERS

Fun Fact

A bittern refers to any of approximately 12 solitary marsh birds in the subfamily Botaurinae within the heron family Ardeidae.

KINGFISHERS THE FLASH OF COLOUR

Kingfishers are colourful birds often found by water bodies. They dive at high speeds to catch fish.

HERONS THE STEALTHY STRIKERS

Herons move slowly to hunt fish and frogs in shallow waters. They strike quickly to catch their prey.

GREBES DIVING DANCERS

Grebes are freshwater diving birds. They are known for their fun dances and ability to 'walk' on water.

BITTERNS THE MARSH MASTERS

Bitterns are wetland birds that hide in the reeds. They have loud calls that can be heard over long distances.

RAILS THE HIDDEN RUNNERS

Rails are shy birds that live in dense marshes. They are usually heard, not seen, because they like to hide.

THE DESERT BIRDS

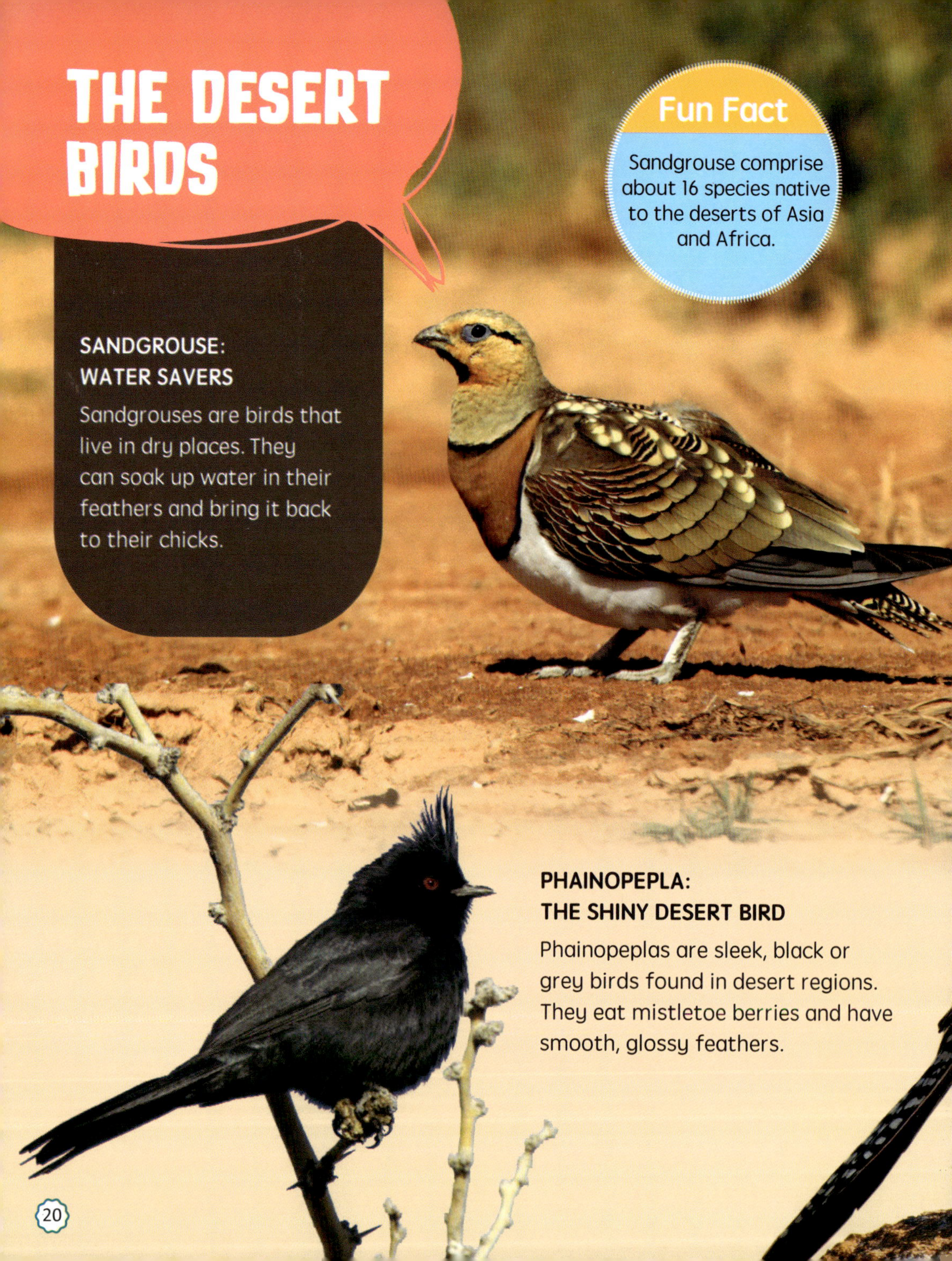

Fun Fact

Sandgrouse comprise about 16 species native to the deserts of Asia and Africa.

SANDGROUSE: WATER SAVERS

Sandgrouses are birds that live in dry places. They can soak up water in their feathers and bring it back to their chicks.

PHAINOPEPLA: THE SHINY DESERT BIRD

Phainopeplas are sleek, black or grey birds found in desert regions. They eat mistletoe berries and have smooth, glossy feathers.

CACTUS WREN: THE DESERT ARCHITECT

Cactus wrens build large, complex nests in cactus plants which provides shelter from the harsh desert environment.

OSTRICH: THE DESERT GIANT

Ostriches are mostly found in African savannahs, but they also live in deserts. They are great at surviving in extreme conditions.

ROADRUNNERS: THE DESERT SPRINTERS

Roadrunners are ground birds that can run up to 27 km per hour, hunting snakes and lizards in the North American deserts.

MIGRATORY MARVELS

SWALLOWS: THE MESSENGERS OF SPRING

Swallows fly thousands of miles between their breeding and wintering grounds. They are celebrated in many cultures as symbols of spring's arrival.

ARCTIC TERNS: THE LONGEST MIGRATION

Arctic terns travel the longest distance of any animal. They fly from the Arctic to the Antarctic and back every year covering 30, 000 kilometres.

Fun Fact

The bar-tailed godwit is one of four large, long-legged, long-billed migratory waders.

SANDHILL CRANES: THE ANCIENT TRAVELLERS

Sandhill cranes are one of the oldest bird species. Their migration is a spectacle involving thousands of birds.

RED KNOTS: A RACE AGAINST TIME

Red knots plan their migration to match when horseshoe crabs lay eggs. They eat the eggs to get energy for their long journey.

BAR-TAILED GODWITS: NON-STOP FLYERS

Bar-tailed godwits hold the record for the longest non-stop flight during migration. They can travel up to 13,500 kilometres without a break.

GRASSLAND BIRDS

THE GREATER PRAIRIE CHICKEN: A BOOMING DISPLAY

They are known for their unique dances and loud calls, which are amplified by air sacs in their necks.

Fun Fact

Secretary birds build large stick nests in low thorny trees, and generally lay one to three eggs.

THE SECRETARY BIRD: GREAT HUNTERS

The secretary bird has long legs and is great at hunting snakes in the African savannas.

SAGE GROUSE: ICONS OF THE SAGEBRUSH

These birds live in sagebrush habitats in North America. They are known for their special displays.

THE KORI BUSTARD: AFRICA'S HEAVYWEIGHT

It is one of the heaviest flying birds and is found in African grasslands. It feeds on on a variety of insects and other small animals.

SKYLARKS: THE SINGING TRAVELLERS

Skylarks are celebrated for their beautiful singing performances. They often sing while flying over European and Asian grasslands.

THE HIGH FLYERS

RÜPPELL'S GRIFFON VULTURE: SOARING THE STRATOSPHERE

This vulture holds the record for the highest flying bird, spotted at altitudes up to 11,300 metres (37,000 feet).

Fun Fact

Bar-headed geese are capable of reducing their metabolic rate to cope with oxygen scarcity.

THE ANDEAN CONDOR: A MASSIVE WINGSPAN

The Andean condor is one of the world's largest flying birds. It has a wingspan reaching up to 3.3 metres (10.8 feet).

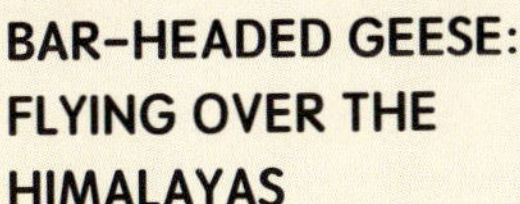

BAR-HEADED GEESE: FLYING OVER THE HIMALAYAS

These geese fly over the Himalayas, high in the sky where the air has much less oxygen than at sea level.

THE ALPINE SWIFT: LIFE IN THE AIR

Alpine swifts can fly for up to six months without landing. They eat and sleep while flying.

THE COMMON CRANE: THE HIGH FLYERS

Common cranes are known for flying long distances. They use thermal currents to help them fly very high.

THE COLOURFUL AND EXOTIC

PEACOCKS: THE PINNACLE OF SHOWMANSHIP

Peacocks are famous for their beautiful tail feathers. They spread them out to impress their partners.

Fun Fact

The resplendent quetzal is considered sacred in many Mesoamerican cultures. It is associated with the 'god of the air' by ancient Mayas and Aztecs.

MACAWS: THE RAINFOREST'S COLOURFUL BIRDS

Macaws are brilliantly coloured parrots from the American tropics. They play vital roles in their habitats as seed dispersers.

THE RESPLENDENT QUETZAL

The quetzal has bright green tail feathers. It is named after the Aztec word for big, shiny feather.

MANDARIN DUCKS

The male mandarin duck helps keep the eggs warm for 28 to 33 days. After the eggs hatch, he leaves, and the mother cares for the ducklings.

THE SCARLET IBIS: A FLUSH OF RED

This strikingly red bird lives in South American wetlands. Its colour comes from the sea creatures it eats.

BIRDS OF THE NIGHT

BARN OWLS: THE SILENT HUNTERS

Barn owls are known for their heart-shaped faces and loud screech. They are common and help control rodent numbers.

THE GREAT HORNED OWL: THE SILENT PREDATOR

Great Horned Owls are strong hunters. They can catch big preys like osprey and peregrine falcons, as well as smaller animals like rodents and frogs.

Fun Fact

The great horned owl is often called the 'tiger of the skies' because it is strong and rulesover other raptors in its territory.

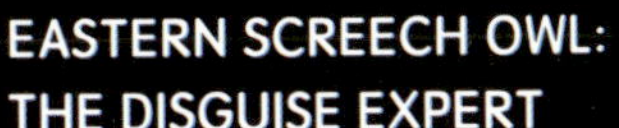

EASTERN SCREECH OWL: THE DISGUISE EXPERT

Small and stocky, these owls are masters of disguise, blending perfectly into their woodland surroundings.

THE TAWNY OWL: THE WOODLAND WATCHER

Tawny owls live in Europe and Asia. They are known for their 'twit-twoo' call, which is often heard in stories and folklore.

NIGHT HERONS: THE TWILIGHT FISHERS

Unlike most herons, night herons are active during the evening and early morning, hunting in the cover of darkness.

THE AQUATIC BIRDS

Fun Fact

Loons have solid bones that help them dive as they don't float as much as other birds.

LOONS: THE NORTHERN DIVERS

These birds are known for their eerie calls and exceptional diving abilities. They are iconic birds of northern lakes.

PELAGIC CORMORANTS: THE SEA'S STALWARTS

These birds are skilled divers and can be seen along rocky coastal waters, diving for fish.

FRIGATEBIRDS: THE PIRATES OF THE SKIES

Frigatebirds are great flyers with big wings. They steal food from other birds while flying and can stay in the air for weeks.

KING EIDERS: ARCTIC SEAFARERS

These are strong sea ducks. They breed in the cold Arctic and spend the winter in tough northern ocean waters.

THE MUTE SWAN: GRACEFUL SWIMMERS

Mute swans are known for being graceful on water. They are strong swimmers and can be quite territorial during the breeding season.

URBAN ADAPTERS

HOUSE FINCHES: THE COLOURFUL INVADERS

Originally from the western United States, house finches have adapted well to cities across the continent.

Fun Fact

European starlings were brought to New York in the early 1890s by a group who wanted to bring all the birds mentioned in Shakespeare's works to America.

EUROPEAN STARLINGS: CITY CONQUERORS

Starlings were introduced to North America in the 1800s. They do well in cities because they can eat different types of food and build nests in different places.

PEREGRINE FALCONS: CITY HUNTERS

Peregrine falcons, once endangered, now live in cities and use tall buildings to catch pigeons.

WHITE-THROATED SPARROWS: CITY SINGERS

These sparrows have changed their tunes in noisy cities. They sing at a higher pitch so their calls can be heard over the noise.

ROCK PIGEONS: THE ORIGINAL CITY BIRD

Rock pigeons have lived alongside humans for thousands of years. They thrive in cities, where tall buildings are like the cliffs they used to live on.

THE ARCTIC SPECIALISTS

SNOWY OWLS: ARCTIC HUNTERS

These majestic birds are among the few predators that thrive in the Arctic's harsh winter, preying mainly on lemmings.

BRÜNNICH'S GUILLEMOTS: CLIFF NESTERS

These seabirds breed on steep cliffs in the Arctic. They dive deep into cold waters to fetch fish for their young.

Fun Fact

The snowy owl's feathered feet help it conserve heat and walk on the snow which acts like natural snowshoes.

ARCTIC TERNS: SUN CHASERS

Famous for their pole-to-pole migrations, these birds see more sunlight than any other during their annual travel.

PTARMIGANS: MASTERS OF HIDING

They change their feathers from brown in summer to pure white in winter. This helps them blend in on the Arctic tundra.

PUFFINS: THE SEA CLOWNS REVISITED

The Atlantic Puffin, the smallest of all puffins, is the sole member of its family living in the Atlantic Ocean.

FOREST FLYERS

SCARLET MACAWS: RAINFOREST FRIENDS

Scarlet macaws show love by touching feet, licking each other's faces, and talking to each other.

Fun Fact

Bald eagles are not actually bald. Their name comes from an old English word, 'balde' which means white, because of their white-feathered heads.

BALD EAGLES: AMERICA'S SYMBOL

Bald eagles are capable of diving at a speed of up to 160 km/h (100 mph).

ASIAN PARADISE FLYCATCHERS: GRACEFUL FLYERS

These flycatchers have long, beautiful tail feathers and are a beautiful sight in Asian forests.

GREAT HORNBILLS: THE JUNGLE GIANTS

These large birds are crucial for the dispersal of many forest seeds in Asian tropical rainforests.

HOOPES: THE CROWNED FLYERS

Hoopes have a special crown of feathers. They are often found in forests across Africa, Europe, and Asia. They feed on insects.

COASTAL BIRDS

MAGNIFICENT FRIGATEBIRDS: NOISY FLYERS

Instead of the usual bird songs, magnificent frigatebirds make sounds, such as drumming, rattling, and clacking .

Fun Fact

Brown pelicans breed in tropical and subtropical coastal colonies along both Atlantic and Pacific shores of the Americas.

OYSTERCATCHERS: THE SHELLFISH SPECIALISTS

Oystercatchers use their strong bills to open shellfish along rocky coastlines.

BROWN PELICANS: DIVING FISHERS

These pelicans are famous for their dramatic plunge dives, snatching up fish in their large throat pouches.

RED KNOTS: COASTAL MARATHONERS

Red knots migrate long distances and stop at the coast to eat horseshoe crab eggs, especially in Delaware Bay.

COMMON MURRES: PENGUIN-LIKE SWIMMERS

These birds dive deep into the water to catch fish. They swim like penguins, even though they can fly.

ISLAND SPECIALISTS

THE DODO

The dodo, a flightless bird from Mauritius, became extinct in the 17th century due to human activities and introduced predators.

HAWAIIAN HONEYCREEPERS: NATURE'S VARIETY

These birds show an amazing variety of forms. Some drink nectar, while others eat seeds, showing how animals change to adapt to their environment.

NEW ZEALAND'S KIWI: THE UNIQUE BIRD

Kiwis are more like mammals than other birds in many ways.

GALÁPAGOS FINCHES: DARWIN'S CLUES

Galápagos finches helped in shaping Darwin's theory of evolution. Each type of finch has a beak specially adapted to its food and surroundings.

SOCOTRA SUNBIRD: THE NECTAR HUNTER

While nectar is the primary component of their diet, Sunbirds also consume fruit, insects, and spiders. Insects are particularly important for feeding their young.

STRUCTURE OF BIRDS

FEATHERED FLYERS

Birds are the only animals in the world with feathers. Their feathers keep them warm in winter and cool in summer. They also protect them from rain and wind. Feathers come in many colours and patterns, helping birds hide from danger or attract a mate. Some birds, like peacocks, have bright and beautiful feathers, while others, like owls, have soft, subtle feathers to help them sneak up on their food.

WARM-BLOODED WONDERS

Birds have warm bodies, even when the weather is very cold. Their body temperature stays between 39–43°C, which is hotter than most other animals. This helps them stay active, fly fast, and search for food. When it's cold outside, birds puff up their feathers like fluffy coats to trap warm air. Some birds, like penguins, huddle together to share warmth. Others, like swallows, fly to warmer places in winter so they don't get too cold.

LIGHT BUT STRONG BONES

Birds have super-light bones that help them fly. Their bones have tiny air spaces inside, making them light like a balloon but still strong. Even big birds, like eagles, have light bones so they can soar high in the sky without getting too heavy. This also helps birds fly long distances without using too much energy. Some birds, like ostriches, don't fly, but they have strong bones to help them run very fast instead.

TOOTHLESS EATERS

Birds don't have teeth like people or other animals. Instead, they have a special stomach part called a gizzard that helps crush their food. Some birds swallow tiny rocks or pebbles, which help the gizzard grind up food, just like teeth do. Hawks have sharp beaks to tear meat, while parrots have strong beaks to crack nuts. Ducks have flat beaks to scoop up food from water.

HUMMING HEARTBEATS

The heart of a tiny hummingbird beats super fast-up to 1,260 times in just one minute when it's flying. That is way faster than a human heart, which beats around 70 times a minute. This fast heartbeat gives hummingbirds lots of energy, so they can flap their wings really quickly; almost 80 times per second. This helps them hover in one place while drinking nectar from flowers. At night, their heart slows down to save energy while they rest.

NESTS

THE NO-NEST BIRDS: NIGHTJARS

Nightjars are special birds because they don't build nests at all. Instead of making a nest with sticks or grass, they simply lay their eggs on the ground, often on leaves or small pebbles. Their eggs have colours that help them blend in with the ground, keeping them safe from hungry animals. The mother bird stays very still, and because her feathers look like the ground, she is almost invisible. This clever trick helps keep her babies safe.

Fun Fact

The largest bald eagle nest ever recorded was 9.5 feet wide.

THE GIANT NEST OF THE BALD EAGLE

Bald eagles build the biggest nests in the world. Their nests can be as wide as a small car-about 5 to 6 feet across-and as tall as a grown-up person; 2 to 4 feet high. These nests are made of sticks and twigs. Some of their nests get so heavy they can weigh more than a motorbike. Eagles like to build their nests high up in tall trees near rivers or lakes so they can easily find fish to eat.

THE MUD-BALL BUILDER: CLIFF SWALLOWS

Cliff swallows are amazing builders. They make their nests out of tiny mud balls, carrying each piece in their beaks. It takes about 1,000 to 1,400 mud balls to finish one nest. The birds stick these little mud balls together to create a round, cosy home that looks like a small cave. Swallows build their nests under bridges, on cliffs, and on buildings. They live in big groups, with lots of nests side by side, just like a bird apartment building.

HUMMINGBIRD'S STICKY SECRET

Hummingbirds make tiny, cosy nests. They use spider webs to hold them together. The silk from the spider's web works like glue, helping the nest stay strong while also making it stretchy. This is important because as baby hummingbirds grow, the nest stretches to fit them. Hummingbird nests are so small that they can fit on a spoon. These tiny birds carefully decorate their nests with bits of moss, leaves, and soft plant fibres to hide them from danger and make them warm.

THE UNDERGROUND NEST OF THE EUROPEAN BEE-EATER

The European bee-eater has a fascinating way to stay cool; it builds its nest underground! These birds dig tunnels in sandy soil, sometimes as deep as 6 feet! At the end of the tunnel, they make a small room where they lay their eggs. The underground nest keeps the eggs and baby birds safe from the hot sun and hungry animals. Since bee-eaters eat bees and insects, their nest is far away from danger, giving their babies a safe place to grow.

Titles in this Series

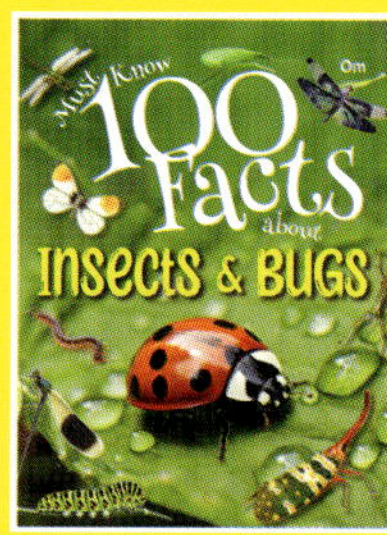

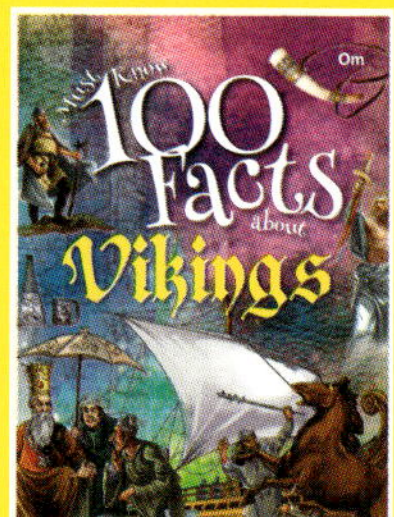

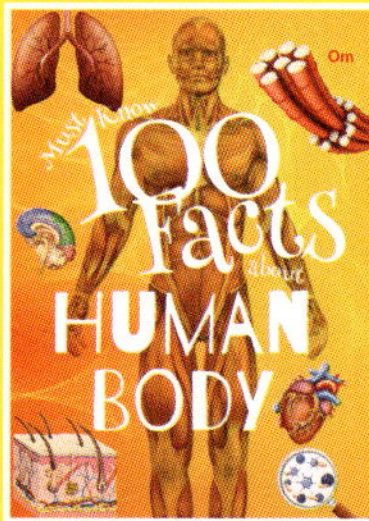

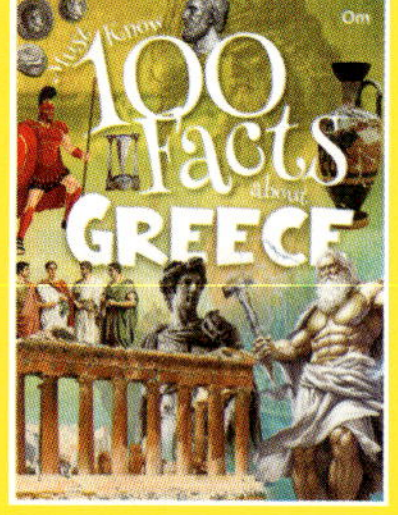

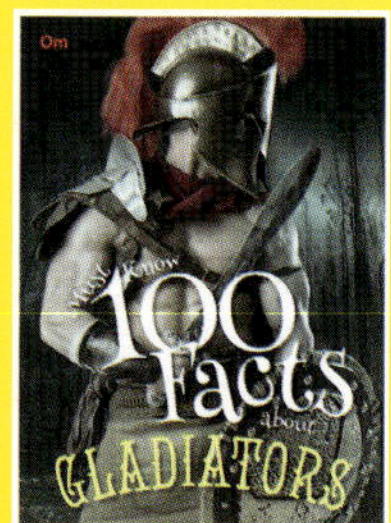

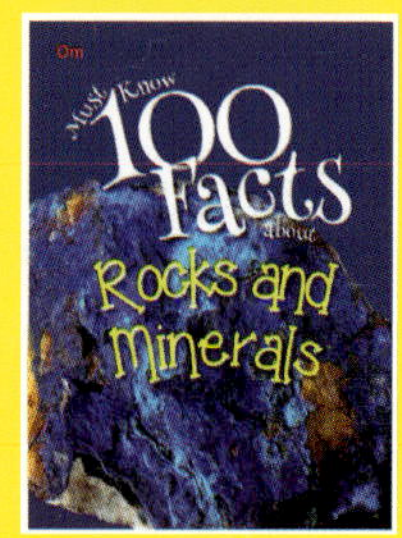